Measuring Weight and Time

© Aladdin Books Ltd 1998
Produced by
Aladdin Books Ltd
28 Percy Street
London W1P OLD

First published in the United States
in 1998 by
Copper Beech Books,
an imprint of
The Millbrook Press
2 Old New Milford Road
Brookfield, Connecticut 06804

Project Editor: Sally Hewitt
Editor: Liz White
Design: David West Children's Books
Designer: Simon Morse
Photography: Roger Vlitos
Illustrator: Tony Kenyon

Printed in Belgium

Library of Congress Cataloging-in-Publication Data
King, Andrew, 1961–
Measuring weight and time / by Andrew King ; illustrated
by Tony Kenyon.
p. cm. — (Math for fun)
Includes index.
Summary: Simple games and activities introduce the concepts of
measuring weight, mass, and time.
ISBN 0-7613-0854-7 (lib. bdg.) —
ISBN 0-7613-0748-6 (pbk.)
1. Weight (Physics)—Measurement—Experiments—Juvenile
literature. 2. Mass (Physics)—Measurement—
Experiments—Juvenile literature. 3. Time
measurements—Experiments—Juvenile literature.
[1. Weight (Physics)—Experiments. 2. Mass
(Physics)—Experiments. 3. Time measurements—
Experiments. 4. Measurement—
Experiments. 5. Experiments.]
I. Kenyon, Tony, ill. II. Title.
III. Series: King, Andrew, 1961–
Math for fun.
QC106.8—K56   98-4229
530.8—dc21   CIP AC

TH *for fun*

Measuring Weight and Time

Andrew King

COPPER BEECH BOOKS
BROOKFIELD, CONNECTICUT

CONTENTS

INTRODUCTION

Everywhere you go you can see clocks, and have you noticed how many objects can be weighed in ounces and pounds? How heavy is an elephant? How many minutes old are you? If you can measure weight and tell the time, you can answer questions like these.

Try the exciting activities, practical projects, and fun games in this book, and you can learn about measuring weight and time.

● Follow the STEP-BY-STEP INSTRUCTIONS to help you with the activities.

● Use the HELPFUL HINTS for clues about the experiments and games.

● Look at MORE IDEAS for information about other projects.

1 Yellow squares mean this is an easy activity.

2 Blue squares mean this is a medium activity.

3 Pink squares mean this is a more difficult activity. You'll have to think hard!

WEIGHT

How heavy is an elephant?
How about a mouse?
How heavy is the lump
of cheese in your refrigerator? We can
measure how heavy things are by weighing
them. Sometimes, the **weight** of an object
is called its **mass**, and we can
measure it in **ounces** (oz) or
pounds (lbs).

SLIMMING SNAKES

Did you know the weight
of an object never changes,
no matter what shape it is?
Make these snakes and find
out for yourself.

2 Roll the play dough with your hands to make a short, fat snake.

1 Choose your favorite play dough color. Measure 5 ounces on a **scale** and roll the play dough into a ball.

3 Put it back on a scale and weigh it again. How much does it weigh now? Yes! Exactly the same... 5 ounces.

4 Keep rolling out the snake. How thin can you make it?

5 Every so often, weigh it again on the scale. It always weighs the same!

HELPFUL HINTS

● Remember that you must not let any part of your snake break off, otherwise the weight will change. This is quite tricky when the snake gets very skinny!

MORE IDEAS

● Weigh out another 5oz of play dough and make another animal, perhaps a dog. Although it looks very different from the snake, they both weigh exactly the same.

● Now make the body of an elephant with your new piece of play dough. Measure out another 3oz of dough of a different color or colors. Use this for the legs, ears, tail, and trunk. What do you think the elephant will weigh? That's right, it will weigh 8 ounces because 5oz + 3oz = 8ozs.

6 It doesn't matter how fat or thin you make the snake, the weight never changes.

POUNDS

Most heavy things in the house, like your mom or dad, are weighed in pounds. Can you find out how many pounds they weigh? How many pounds do you weigh?

HOW MANY?
You can play this guessing game with your friends. Do you know how many ounces make one pound? It's sixteen! This can be written in figures like this...

16 oz = 1 lb

1 First, decide what you are going to weigh. You need to **estimate** how many of each item it will take to make 1 pound. Make scorecards for each of your friends and write down your estimates.

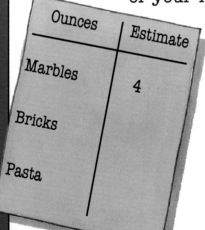

Ounces	Estimate
Marbles	4
Bricks	
Pasta	

2 Now collect the objects to weigh and the scale you are going to measure with.

3 If you are estimating the number of marbles needed to make 1 pound, then take turns with your friends to keep adding one more marble at a time... and watch the weight slowly rise!

4 When the scale shows 1lb, stop and count the number of marbles on the scale. The player that made the best guess is the winner!

HELPFUL HINTS

● If you are measuring with a bathroom scale, you will need a lightweight container to hold the things you are weighing.

● To be good at this game, it helps to get a feeling for a pound. Take a look in your kitchen cabinet. Sugar, rice, and other foods are often sold in weights of 1lb. Make sure you ask an adult before you start looking!

MORE IDEAS

● Now that you are good at estimating the numbers of different things that make 1lb, you can play Combo Crazy! Choose any two of the objects you have been weighing. Can you combine some pasta and marbles to make 1lb? How close can you get to a pound?

OUNCES

Which is heavier: an ounce of feathers or an ounce of nails? They are both the same! The feathers take up more space, but they weigh the same. If something is large, it doesn't mean that it is always heavier than something small. If you remember this, it will help you to play human scale.

HUMAN SCALE

1 Choose about ten things from around the house. What about a cushion, a cup, a book... perhaps you can think of some other interesting items. Write the name of each object on a piece of paper.

2 Now you need to be a human scale! Which do you think is the heaviest object? Put it on the right-hand side of the table.

3 Which do you think is the lightest? Place that on the left. Can you put everything else in order, from lightest to heaviest?

4 Now you can find out how good you are as a human scale! Start with what you think is the lightest object and weigh it on a scale. How many ounces does it weigh?

Shoe   7oz

Cushion   6oz

Cup   5oz

5 Write the weight on a card and put it next to the card of the object.

6 Do the same for all the other objects. How good were you at getting everything in order?

HELPFUL HINTS

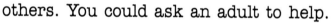

● There are lots of different scales you could use. Some are easier to understand than others. You could ask an adult to help.

● If you use a kitchen scale, you can choose light and heavy objects. When using a bathroom scale, choose heavier objects only.

MORE IDEAS

● You can play another game like this with old containers. Measure 2oz, 3oz, 4oz, 5oz, 6oz, and 8oz of rice into six containers. Cover each with a paper napkin that can be held in place with a rubber band. Mark each with a letter so you know which is which. Write down the answers on a piece of paper and hide it. Then challenge your friends to get them in the correct order from heaviest to lightest.

HUNT THE OZ

Many things in stores are sold in different weights. Take a look next time you visit. Watch out for the letters "oz" next to some numbers. This is short for ounces and is one of the ways that we can measure weight.

POPPING CORN! Have you ever eaten popcorn? That's right, the light, fluffy-looking stuff.

1 Have you ever seen popcorn before it is popped? The grains are small, tough, and yellow. You will need some popcorn and a scale to try this experiment.

2 What do you think will happen to the weight of the popcorn once it has popped? Will it get lighter, heavier, or stay the same?

3 You will need an adult to help you cook the popcorn. Get a large pan with a lid. Put a teaspoon of vegetable oil in the bottom of the pan and warm it on a low heat.

4 Put 3oz of popcorn into the pan and put the lid on! Keep moving the pan gently and listen to the popcorn popping!

5 When there are hardly any more pops, take the pan off the heat and lift the lid carefully — **remember it is still very hot.**

6 Before you start eating, weigh it again. The strange thing is that although each piece feels very light, the popcorn weighs exactly the same as it did before!

HELPFUL HINTS

● If you don't have this type of scale, you could put the popcorn in a paper bag and weigh it on a bathroom scale.

● Many scales can be adjusted so when the bowl is placed on top, zero ounces is registered.

MORE IDEAS

● Weigh a large potato. How many ounces does it weigh? What do you think will happen if the potato is boiled? Why not try freezing the potato and see if that affects the weight!

KITCHEN COUNTERS

Did you know that cooks need to be very good at arithmetic? Look at a cookbook. The instructions for making a dish usually have some **measurements**. Some are about the amount of time needed to cook the ingredients, and others show the quantities of the ingredients.

COOKIE BAKING
This is a simple recipe for making 40 scrumptious cookies! You will need an adult to help you.

1 Grease a cookie sheet with a thin film of butter. Preheat the oven to 350 degrees Fahrenheit.

2 Weigh 7oz of butter, 7oz of sugar, and 10$\frac{1}{2}$oz of all-purpose flour and put them in separate bowls. You also need an egg.

3 Put the butter and sugar into a mixing bowl and beat together well with a wooden spoon until the mixture looks creamy.

4 Add the egg to the mixture and beat well. Add the flour and carefully mix it in.

6 You should be able to make about 40 cookies from this mixture. Place them about $1\frac{1}{2}$ inches apart.

5 Take a small piece of the mixture the size of a large nut. Roll it into a ball. Place the ball on the cookie sheet and gently press to flatten it.

HELPFUL HINTS

● The mixture can get quite sticky! After you have washed and dried your hands, cover them with a little flour before you start to roll the mixture into balls.
● Be careful when you take the cookie sheet out of the oven. Remember it is still hot.

MORE IDEAS

● If you are making your cookies for a party, why don't  you decorate them with some icing? Weigh $3\frac{1}{2}$oz of confectioners sugar, add a teaspoon of water, and beat well. Spread the icing thinly on the cookies and then add some of your favorite candy on top!

7 Put the cookie sheet in the oven and bake for about 15 minutes, or until the cookies are golden brown. Use a spatula to move them to a wire rack until they are cool enough to eat... enjoy!

WEIGHTY PROBLEMS

The best way of tackling a weighty problem is to begin by making a careful guess, or estimate, of the answer. As you try to find the answer, make a note of the calculations you do. It can be easy to make a mistake, and if you have written things down it is easy to check back.

WORTH YOUR WEIGHT IN GOLD
There is a famous legend that a prince was rewarded by the king with his weight in gold.

If you were rewarded for being good by having your weight in chocolate, how many bars would you get?

1 You could begin by choosing your favorite bar of chocolate. Guess how much it weighs — don't look at the wrapper yet.

Candy Store

2 Now weigh yourself. How many pounds are you?

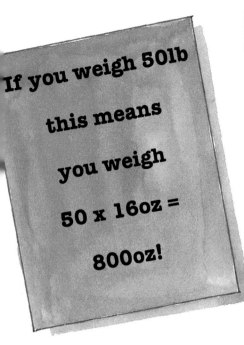

If you weigh 50lb this means you weigh 50 x 16oz = 800oz!

3 Next, change the pounds you weigh into ounces. Do you remember that 1lb = 16oz?

4 Now find the weight of the chocolate bar printed on the wrapper. Divide your weight in ounces by the weight of the bar in ounces. You could use a calculator to help you.

If your bar weighs 1.5oz, this is the number of bars you would get.

533.3334

Ignore these numbers after the decimal point.

MORE IDEAS

● How hungry are you in the morning? Do you like a big breakfast — a really BIG breakfast? Lions do. They usually like a one-course meal of wildebeest, and can eat half their own weight in three days.

● Find out how much your breakfast weighs altogether. Do you have a lion-sized appetite? How long would it take you to eat half your weight?

TIME

Who is the fastest? How long does it take to travel into town? Since the beginning of time people have been trying to measure **time**! In the past people used other ways of measuring time. They looked at shadows made by the sun on sun dials, and at night they watched the speed at which candles melted to measure time.

DRIP, DROP, TICK, TOCK
One way you can measure time is by using a water clock. You can make your own water clock to measure exactly one minute.

1 Find a large glass jar and stick a white strip of paper to the side like this.

2 Find an old dishwashing liquid bottle with a cap, and carefully cut off the bottom half. You will need an adult to help you with this.

3 Make sure you have a clock with a second hand ready.

4 Put some play dough at the neck of the bottle. Make a small hole in it. Make sure the cap is screwed on tightly. Fill the bottle with water from the bottom.

5 Hold it over the jar. When you are ready, take off the cap so the water starts to trickle into the jar. After one minute, mark on the paper the level the water has reached in the jar.

6 If the water is still running through after two minutes, make another mark. When it has finished, you have made a water clock that you can fill with water and use as a timer.

MORE IDEAS
● You can play dress-up races using your water clock as a timer!
● See if you can find an old hat, shirt, pants, and some of your mom or dad's shoes. Can you or your friends put them on before the water trickles through up to the minute mark?

MEASURING TIME

How many different watches or clocks are there in your house? What do they have in common? Clocks usually have a short hour hand and a long minute hand. Some may have a second hand, too. We measure time in seconds, minutes, and hours.

TIME FLIES

You can play this game with a friend. The object is to start your clock at 6 o'clock and be the first to reach 9 o'clock.

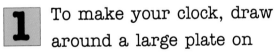

1 To make your clock, draw around a large plate on some cardboard and cut it out. Copy the hours from this example onto your circle.

2 To make the hands, cut out two strips of cardboard. Make one longer than the other. Use a paper fastener to push through the hands and the center of the clock face. Set the hands to 6 o'clock.

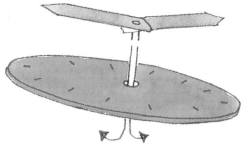

3 Think up activities that take 5, 10, 20, or 30 minutes. Make 25 cards and write the different activities and times on them.

5 mins. brush teeth

10 mins. take a bath

20 mins. walk the dog

30 mins. do homework

4 Take turns to take a card from the pile. Move your clock hands around the amount of minutes shown on the card. The first to reach 9 o'clock wins the game.

JUST A MINUTE

"Just a minute..." "Wait a minute." People use sayings like these all the time, but why does a minute never seem the same length as the minute you are thinking of?

A minute is the same as sixty seconds — that's easy to remember! But it doesn't always help us to feel how long a minute is!

TIME UP

This is a good game to help you feel how long a minute is. You can play the game with two or more friends. You will need a watch with a second hand.

1 The player in charge of the watch says "Go!" The other players have to guess when they think a minute is over.

2 When you think a minute has passed, you must raise your hand high in the air.

3 When the minute is over, the person with the watch shouts "Time is over." The people who have not already raised their hands are out.

4 The winner is the last person to raise a hand before the minute is over.

HELPFUL HINTS

● The second hand on a clock is the one that moves the quickest. When the hand has moved around a full circle, one minute has passed.

● Sometimes, it is easiest to start timing the minute when the second hand reaches the 12, and then stop when it comes around to the 12 again.

● It may be hard to count out a minute in your head. It can help if you add a long word, like "elephant," in between each number you count. If you count "one elephant, two elephant, three elephant" this might help you to count seconds more accurately.

WHAT DID YOU DO TODAY?

Why do parents always want to know what you've been doing at school? Don't they know that after a hard day all you want to do is play! Some people keep a note of the activities they do each day in a book called a **diary**.

ACTIVITY WALLCHART
You could chart what you do each day in a diary and turn it into a colorful wallchart. You will need some cardboard, paper, scissors, pens, and a ruler.

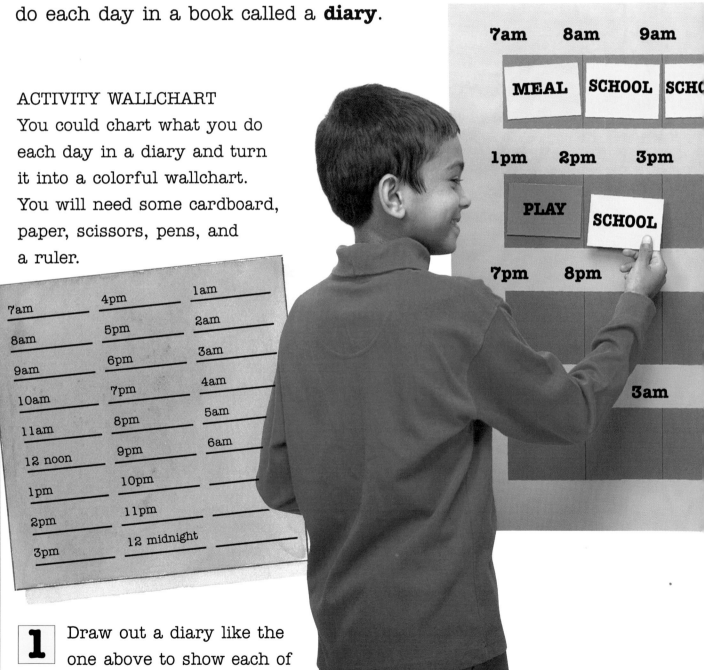

7am	8am	9am
MEAL	SCHOOL	SCHO

1pm	2pm	3pm
PLAY	SCHOOL	

7pm	8pm	

3am

7am	4pm	1am
8am	5pm	2am
9am	6pm	3am
10am	7pm	4am
11am	8pm	5am
12 noon	9pm	6am
1pm	10pm	
2pm	11pm	
3pm	12 midnight	

1 Draw out a diary like the one above to show each of the 24 hours in one day.

2 As you go through your day, fill out your diary with the activities you do during each hour.

3 Make about 35 small cards and choose some activities. Then write the activities on the cards. You might want to write "sleep" on ten of them, "watch t.v." on five, "play" on five, "meal" on five, and "school" on ten. Can you think of any others?

WATCH T.V.

SLEEP

PLAY

MEAL

SCHOOL

11am   12noon   1pm

AY   SCHOOL   MEAL

5pm   6pm

12am

4 Find a large piece of cardboard for your wallchart and draw on it 24 smaller squares — one square for each hour of your diary. Label each square with the hour time. Stick the chart onto your wall. Check with an adult first.

5 Now go through your diary and for each hour stick the correct activity card onto your wallchart.

6 When you have finished your 24 hours, you can see how much time you spent sleeping that day. How much time did you spend at school? How about playing?

DIGITAL CLOCKS

Some clocks and watches don't have a face and hands. The time is shown in numbers, or **digits**. Usually the first two digits show the hour, and the last two the minutes. These are called digital clocks.

STOP THE CLOCK

1 Can you arrange some matchsticks to make a time as close to the deadline as possible? Ask an adult before you use the matchsticks.

2 You could draw a guide for your matchsticks like this.

3 You could begin by just trying to make some different times with your matchsticks. This is how you can make eleven minutes before eight, or 07:49.

06.00

17

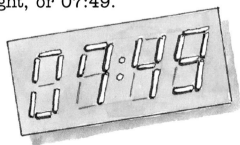

4 Make one pile of cards and write numbers on them from 17 to 21.

5 Make another pile of cards and write some times on them, for example 06.00.

6 You and a friend must each pick a card from the first pile. This will show you how many sticks you can use to make the time.

7 Now choose one time card. You must both try to arrange your sticks as near to this time as possible. The person nearest wins.

HELPFUL HINTS

● If you find it hard to remember what the digits on a clock look like, then use a calculator to remind you — the numbers look the same.

MORE IDEAS

● You could even use the 24-hour clock. A time like one o'clock in the afternoon is shown as `13:00` hours and ten o'clock at night is `22:00` hours.

SECONDS, MINUTES, HOURS...

How long does it take you to get to school? One minute, 15 minutes? You might say it took 900 seconds, but that would seem a little strange! There are many different measurements of time.

When we describe how long something takes, we try to use a measurement that others find easy to understand and that isn't overly exact.

HOW OLD ARE YOU?
No! not years old. That's too easy. How many hours old are you? There is a way that you can find out. You will need a calculator to help you.

1 Multiply your age by the number of days in a year. If you are 9 it would look like this.

9 x 365 = 3,285 days

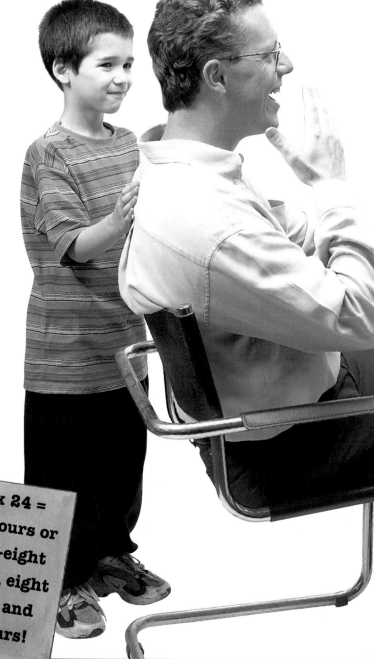

2 Now multiply the answer 3,285, by the number of hours in a day.

3,285 x 24 = 78,840 hours or Seventy-eight thousand, eight hundred and forty hours!

3 Make a birthday card for your mom, dad, brother, or sister, with their age in hours on the front. Find out how many years old they will be next birthday.

35 years old
in hours
―――――――
35 years x
365 days x
24 hours =
―――――――
306,600 hours

4 Then all you have to do is follow the same calculation. Multiply the number of years by 365, and then the answer to that by 24.

HAPPY
BIRTHDAY
DAD
YOU ARE
306,600
HOURS
OLD TODAY

5 Thank goodness you are only making a card and not a cake for their birthday with all those candles!

MORE IDEAS
● If you want to sound very clever, you can estimate the number of minutes old someone is. A quick way to do this, is to halve the person's age and add a million on the end! So, if your friend is 10 years old, then a good estimate is that they are 5 million minutes old.

8 years old
in minutes is
8 ÷ 2 = 4
add six zeros =
―――――――
4,000,000
minutes old

TIME AND WEIGHT

Time

60 seconds = 1 minute

60 minutes = 1 hour

24 hours = 1 day

Weight

16 ounces = 1 pound

2000 pounds = 1 ton

24-hour clock

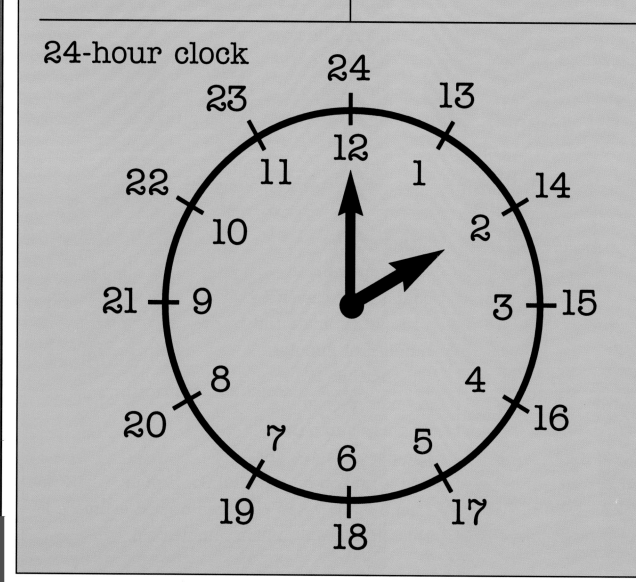

GLOSSARY

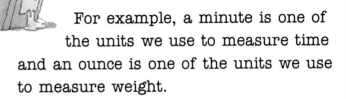

Diary

A diary is a book where you can keep a record of what you do each day. It is usually divided into the days, weeks, and months of one whole year.

Digit

Numbers are made up of digits. There are two digits in the number 25: a 2 and a 5. There are three digits in the number 683: a 6, an 8, and a 3.

Estimate

An estimate is a careful guess. You could estimate how much you think a bag of apples weighs. You can check your estimate by weighing the bag.

Mass

Mass describes how much there is of something. Mass is sometimes used as another word for weight. It is often measured in ounces.

Measurement

We make all kinds of measurements — how far, how heavy, how fast, how long, how high, and so on. We use different units of measurement according to what we are measuring.

For example, a minute is one of the units we use to measure time and an ounce is one of the units we use to measure weight.

Ounce

One of the ways of measuring weight is in ounces. An ounce is a unit of weight or mass. A bar of chocolate weighs about one ounce. There are 16 ounces in a pound.

Scale

A scale is a machine we use for measuring how much things weigh. A kitchen scale measures lightweight things such as an apple, and a bathroom scale can measure heavy things like your mom and dad.

Time

Time is a way of measuring how long it takes for something to happen. You can tell that time is passing by the sun moving across the sky. We use clocks and watches to measure time in seconds, minutes, and hours.

Weight

The weight of an object is how heavy it is. We can pick up a bag of groceries and say whether it seems heavy to us. We use scales to measure exactly how much it weighs in ounces and pounds.

INDEX